CONTENTS

DARWIN'S EARTHWORMS

What do you think this could be?

Charles Darwin studied earthworm's lives and built a **wormstone** like this on his lawn to measure how much soil the worms brought up into the lawn. He studied it for over thirty years!

Charles Darwin was a famous naturalist who died over 100 years ago

Worms spend most of their life in burrows.

Worms pull dead leaves down into their burrows. They also eat pieces of dead leaf and earth. They leave **worm casts** on the surface.

Darwin discovered some incredible facts about worms:

- In 30 years worms buried every stone on a stony field.
- In 2000 years they buried the floor of a Roman villa several metres deep.
- In making their burrows, worms move about 40 tonnes of soil per hectare in a year. Imagine tossing 40 tonnes of soil into and out of a barrow!

In October 1881 Charles Darwin published a book about worms. On the last page he wrote: 'The plough is one of the most ancient and valuable of man's inventions; but long before people existed the land was in fact regularly ploughed, and still continues to be thus ploughed by earthworms.'

> What do you think would happen if all the earthworms in a garden were killed? Would the gardener be happy?

BREAKING THE CHAIN

On the island of Mauritius, where the Dodo bird once lived, there is a kind of tree called the Calvaria. People began to notice that there were no young trees anywhere, only old ones. Why should a tree suddenly stop growing in a place where it had always done so well?

What can we do to stop anything like this needing to be done again?

Bring back the

North American turkeys were sent in! The turkeys ate the fruit, and seeds from the fruit appeared in their droppings. The seeds **germinated** and grew into trees. So now there are turkeys living in Mauritius and new young Calvaria trees are growing there again.

Somebody checked back and found that there had been no seedlings since the fateful time when the last of the poor, flightless Dodos had been hunted down and killed by the greedy settlers who had come to the island. Could there be a connection? It was a mystery!

Dodo

Trees spread their seeds in a variety of ways. One way is for their fruit to be eaten by an animal or bird, carried away in the animal's gut and then grow where the droppings fall. If the Dodo had been the one to do this for this tree, then it would become extinct too unless a Dodo substitute could be found.

TURTLES

All these animals are sea turtles. Although they belong to the same group of animals they are not all the same. Look at the pictures. In what ways are they the same? In what ways are they different?

Loggerhead turtles come furthest north and have occasionally been caught off the coast of Britain. They eat shellfish, crabs, and fish.

The female turtles lay about 150 eggs on the shore. When they have finished laying the eggs, they cover them with sand and head back out to sea, leaving the young to hatch and fend for themselves on the beach.

When the young turtles hatch they are about 5 cm long. They make straight for the sea. On the way to the sea they are likely to be eaten by sea birds, so they usually make this journey at night. All the same, a lot of them are eaten. Only one in a hundred young turtles survive to become adults.

Hawksbill turtles almost became extinct, because their shells make very attractive combs, jewellery, and small boxes.

Atlantic Ridley turtles can sleep on the water but will dive when disturbed. A single breath lasts them a whole hour!

Leatherback turtles are the largest kind of turtle there is. They can weigh over 600 kg. They have a leathery skin instead of a horny outer shell.

Sea turtles cannot withdraw into their shells. For defence they rely on their size and swimming speed.

DESIGNS FROM NATURE

Artists have often been inspired by natural designs –
but so have scientists and engineers. Here are some
of the designs which people copied from plants.

maple fruit

helicopter

dandelion fruit

parachute

lighthouse

oak tree trunk

burdock fruit

Velcro

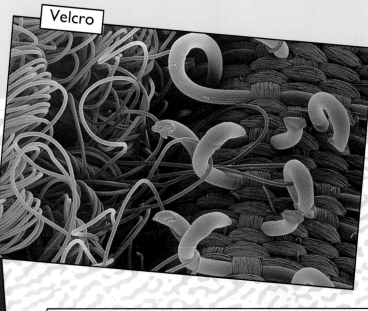

The palm house on page 14 is copied from a water lily leaf! Can you think of other designs?

AS LIKE AS TWO PEAS?

You may look just like your Mum, or have big ears like uncle Ben, but have you ever wondered why?

Why do you think tomato seeds grow into tomatoes and not into strawberries or gooseberries?

Plants and animals can make copies of themselves by **reproducing.**

Both parents pass on chemical instructions called **genes**. Some genes are more powerful, or dominant, than others. The way genes are passed from one generation of plants or animals to another is called **heredity**.

Look at these pictures of cats. Can you work out which cats are the parents of which kittens?

Over a hundred years ago lived an Austrian monk called Gregor Mendel. He studied pea plants to find out which ones produced new young plants with green peas and which ones had yellow peas.

After many years Mendel was able to start to explain how nature's rules of heredity worked.

How do you think gardeners and vegetable growers have used their knowledge of these rules?

Stop thief!

Inspector Clued-Up investigates the bird table mystery

Who stole the bacon off the bird table?

When was the bacon last seen?

I put it out after dinner last night

list of suspects
sparrows   cats
starlings   dogs
tits   foxes
swallows hedgehogs
ducks squirrels
chaffinches finch
hawks blackbirds
merlin thrushes
owls

12

Now who had the motive?

Were all the suspects active at the time?

Did anyone have an alibi?

How would the thief get up there?

Will the thief strike again?

I think I know who did it Do you?

A VISIT TO KEW GARDENS

The palm house at Kew.

When you walk into the Royal Botanic Gardens at Kew it is hard to believe that you are near London. Its 300 acres include different trees and other plants from all over the world. In its vast greenhouses you can see bananas growing, tropical palms, and even sea gardens!

The **botanists** at Kew study plants and find species which will be of use to people everywhere. They rescue and grow rare and endangered plants for return to the wild. They find out what the local people in different parts of the world know about the local plants. They share their knowledge of plants with other people round the world.

Inside the palm house.

Researchers from Kew, like Gail Bromley, collect specimens and seeds for examination and identification. She describes an expedition to North-east Brazil. 'We went collecting with three Brazilian botanists and found many new species. I counted seven new species in one place in one afternoon. When we found an interesting plant we took a small sample and pressed it between sheets of paper, writing notes about its height and colour, what else was growing with it and where we found it. Sometimes we took photographs. We were always careful to leave plenty of the same plants behind.'

We must leave collecting plants like this to the experts! Why shouldn't you pick wild flowers?

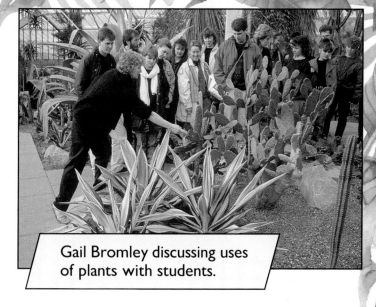

Gail Bromley discussing uses of plants with students.

It is important to be able to identify plants from all over the world. Doctors at the Great Ormond Street children's hospital found that many of their patients were recovering from **eczema**, and at first they didn't know why. Then they discovered that the children were also being treated with Chinese herbs. Experts at Kew examined the herbs and found out what they were. They are now trying to find out what the useful ingredients are so that western doctors can use the same medicine.

Pressing plants.

This cactus came from Brazil.

GROUPS OF LIVING THINGS

Scientists group living things in sets like this.

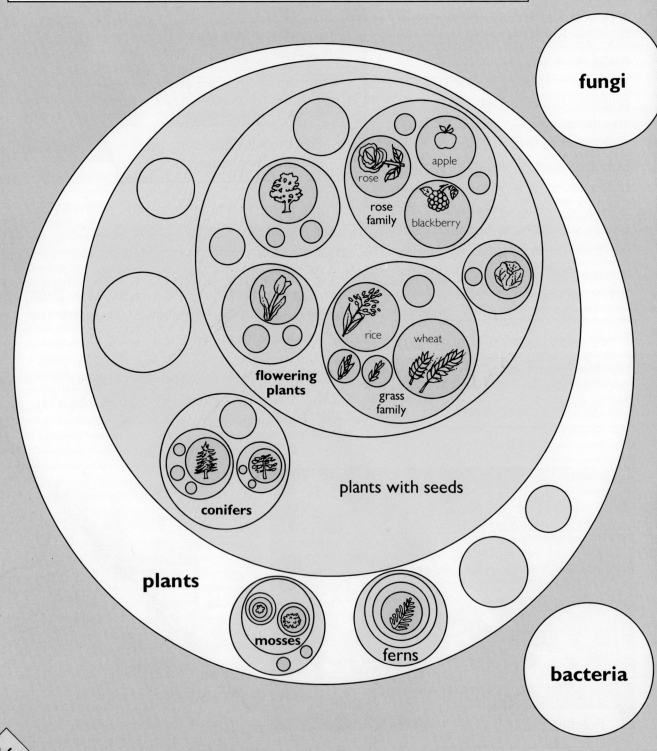

fungi

rose

apple

rose
family

blackberry

flowering
plants

rice

wheat

grass
family

conifers

plants with seeds

plants

mosses

ferns

bacteria

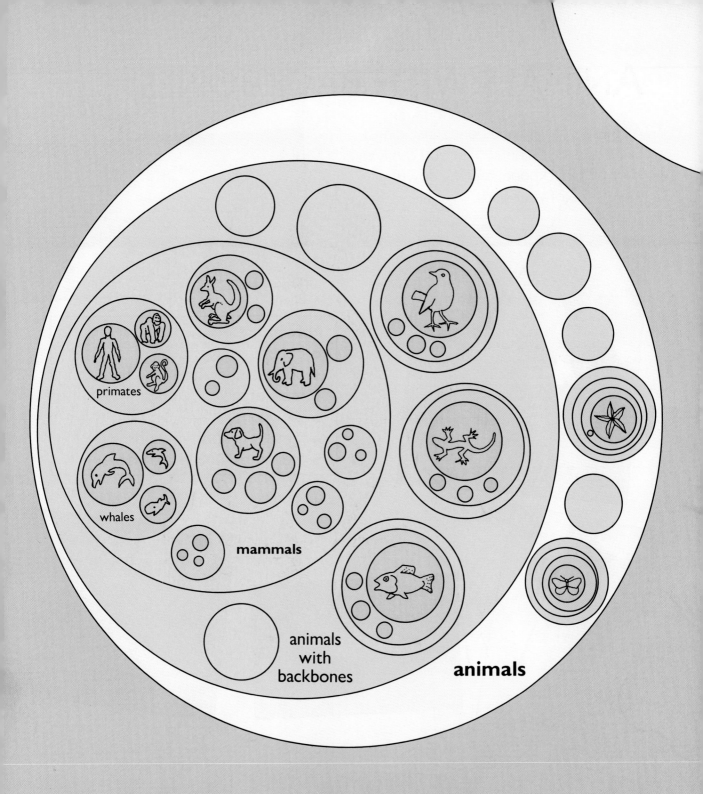

primates

whales

mammals

animals with backbones

animals

all living things

Can you think of other living things that would fit into each of the sets?

17

ANIMALS WITH BACKBONES

All these animals have bones, including a backbone. If you bend over you can feel your own backbone, running down the middle of your back.

Mammal
- bones
- body temperature stays the same
- most of them live on land
- live young
- females produce milk for young
- four limbs (not always visible)

Fish
- bones
- lives in water
- lays eggs in water

Amphibian
- bones
- lives in water when young, adults live on land
- lays eggs in water
- four limbs

Bird
- bones
- body temperature stays same
- most of them live on land
- lays eggs on land
- four limbs (two are wings)
- feathers

Reptile
- bones
- normally lives on land
- lays eggs on land

Can you match up these animals with the group descriptions?

Which ones are difficult to match up?

Are there any that don't match the descriptions?

ANIMALS WITHOUT BACKBONES

Many animals have soft bodies with
no bones. Some have hard shells.

Jellyfish
- jelly-like bag
- mouth surrounded
  by tentacles

Spider
- body in 2 parts
- 4 pairs of legs

Mollusc
- hard shell
- muscular digging or
  swimming foot

Worm
- soft body
- many segments
- no legs

Crustacean
- hard coverings
- segmented bodies
- jointed limbs

Insect
- jointed legs, usually 3 pairs
- body in 3 sections
- antennae

Can you match up these animals with the descriptions?
Are some difficult to match up?

Choose some other animals and see which descriptions match them.
Are there any that don't match?

Starfish/Sea urchin
- more than two sides the same (often five sides)

Centipede/Millipede
- body in many parts
- one or two pairs of legs to each part
- front claws or jaws

21

(These pictures are not all drawn to the same scale.)

PLANTS AND FUNGI

The classification of plants and fungi is very complicated, and scientists do not all agree on how it should be done.

Most plants are green. They use energy from sunlight to make the food they need to build plant cells.

Flowering plants have roots, a stem, leaves, and flowers. Some of these plants are trees. Seeds develop from the flowers and when the seeds are scattered they grow into new plants.

Cone-bearing plants (conifers) are all trees. They have needle-like leaves. Their cones contain seeds which develop into new plants.

Mosses are small, low growing, creeping plants that live in moist shady places. They grow from spores.

Ferns also grow in moist places. They have complicated leaves, roots, and stems. They also grow from spores.

Fungi do not use sunlight to make food. They are not green. Instead they feed on plants, dead or dying, or even on live animals. They **reproduce** by spores.

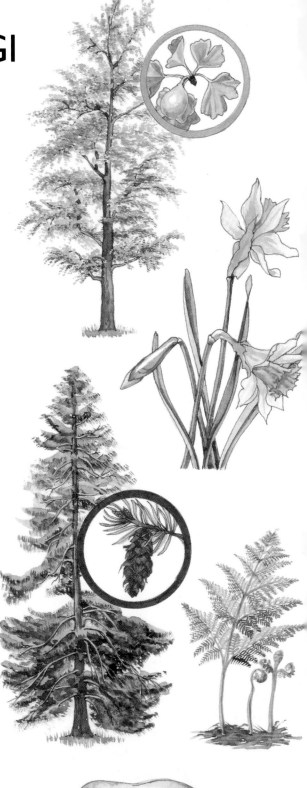

Which of these living things are fungi and which are plants?
Which plants match up with the group descriptions?

Choose some other plants and find out which descriptions they match up with.

Are there any plants which don't match any of the descriptions?

(These pictures are not all drawn to the same scale.)

GLOSSARY

Botanist
A botanist is a person who studies plants.

Extinct
An animal or plant is extinct if there is no living thing of that kind left alive.

Eczema
A person with eczema has patches of sore, itchy skin which often blisters. Eczema isn't catching. It may be caused by dust, soaps, or some kinds of food.

Gene
A gene is a chemical in an animal or plant which is inherited from its parent. Genes are partly responsible for what a living thing looks like.

Germinate
When a seed germinates, a shoot and a root sprout from it and start to grow.

germinating broad bean

Heredity
The way in which genes are passed from one generation of plants or animals, including humans, to another.

Reproduce
When a plant or animal reproduces it produces young or offspring similar to itself.

Wormstone
A wormstone can be used to measure how much soil worms bring up to the surface of the ground.

wormstone

Worm cast
A worm cast is a coil of earth on the surface of the ground. It has been left behind by a burrowing earthworm, after it has passed through the earthworm's body.